Bo and Zop
learn how to be an
EARTHLING

HOW DO EARTHLINGS HELP EACH OTHER?

by Kirsty Holmes

CRABTREE
PUBLISHING COMPANY

Author: Kirsty Holmes

Editorial director: Kathy Middleton

Editors: Madeline Tyler, Janine Deschenes

Proofreader: Melissa Boyce

Graphic design: Dan Scas

**Production coordinator
 & Prepress technician:** Ken Wright

Print coordinator: Katherine Berti

Images

All images are courtesy of Shutterstock.com, unless otherwise specified.

Alien Bo: delcarmat. Alien Zop: Roi and Roi. Background – PremiumArt. Vectors throughout: kearia.

Speech bubbles: Surrphoto.

All facts, statistics, web addresses and URLs in this book were verified as valid and accurate at time of writing. No responsibility for any changes to external websites or references can be accepted by either the author or publisher.

Library and Achives Canada Cataloguing in Publication

Title: How do earthlings help each other? / Kirsty Holmes.
Other titles: Helping others
Names: Holmes, Kirsty, author.
Description: Series statement: Bo & Zop learn how to be an earthling |
  Originally published under title: Helping others: a book about giving.
  King's Lynn: BookLife, 2020. | Includes index.
Identifiers: Canadiana (print) 20200225405 |
  Canadiana (ebook) 20200225413 |
  ISBN 9780778781196 (hardcover) |
  ISBN 9780778781233 (softcover) |
  ISBN 9781427125699 (HTML)
Subjects: LCSH: Helping behavior—Juvenile literature. | LCSH: Help-seeking
  behavior—Juvenile literature. | LCSH: Generosity—Juvenile literature. |
  LCSH: Conduct of life—Juvenile literature.
Classification: LCC BF637.H4 .H65 2021 | DDC j302/.14—dc23

Library of Congress Cataloging-in-Publication Data

Names: Holmes, Kirsty, author.
Title: How do earthlings help each other? / Kirsty Holmes.
Description: New York : Crabtree Publishing Company, 2021. |
  Series: Bo & Zop learn how to be an earthling | Includes index.
Identifiers: LCCN 2020016380 (print) | LCCN 2020016381 (ebook) |
  ISBN 9780778781196 (hardcover) |
  ISBN 9780778781233 (paperback) |
  ISBN 9781427125699 (ebook)
Subjects: LCSH: Social service--Juvenile literature. | Charity--Juvenile
  literature. | Humanitarianism--Juvenile literature.
Classification: LCC HV40 .H6358 2021 (print) | LCC HV40 (ebook) |
  DDC 361--dc23
LC record available at https://lccn.loc.gov/2020016380
LC ebook record available at https://lccn.loc.gov/2020016381

Crabtree Publishing Company

www.crabtreebooks.com   1-800-387-7650

Published by Crabtree Publishing Company in 2021

©2020 BookLife Publishing Ltd

Printed in the U.S.A./072020/CG20200429

Published in Canada
Crabtree Publishing
616 Welland Avenue
St. Catharines, Ontario
L2M 5V6

Published in the United States
Crabtree Publishing
347 Fifth Ave
Suite 1402-145
New York, NY 10016

CONTENTS

Bo and Zop
learn how to be an
EARTHLING

Words with lines underneath, like this, can be found in the glossary on page 24.

SOMEWHERE IN THE SOLAR SYSTEM...

Can you see that bright light in the night sky? What is it? It could be a star. It could be a <u>satellite</u>. Or it could be... an alien spaceship!

Earth

Alien spaceship

Two brave aliens from planet Omegatron are on a mission to planet Earth. Their names are Bo and Zop. They want to learn all about Earthlings before they decide if Earth is safe to visit.

"I'm Zop! And... Bo, are you okay in there?"

"I'm Bo. I can't talk right now."

Oh dear! Bo is trying to clean his room, but it is a big challenge. The mess is not getting any better. In fact, it is starting to get a lot worse.

Bo doesn't want any help. He wants to show Zop that he can do things by himself. But Zop knows everyone needs some help sometimes. He has been studying how Earthlings help each other.

How do you help other Earthlings?

"Bo, it is okay to ask for help!"

7

EARTHLINGS HAVE NEEDS

Earthlings have <u>basic</u> needs that must be met. They need these things to survive, or stay alive.

Food

Water

Air

Shelter

Earthlings have other needs too. These things help them stay healthy and happy.

safety

Health care

Education

Love

HELPING AND GIVING

Sometimes, Earthlings cannot meet their needs. This could happen for many reasons.

"Earthlings all over the world need help sometimes."

Poverty

NO WORKERS REQUIRED

Losing their job

Becoming unwell

Dealing with natural disasters

Luckily, Earthlings can be really good at helping each other. There are many ways that Earthlings help others meet their needs.

They can share <u>goods</u>.

They can <u>donate</u> money.

They can <u>volunteer</u> their time.

WORKING TOGETHER

Earthlings know that working together helps them solve big problems. By adding their time, ideas, and money together, Earthlings can help many others.

These Earthlings work together to make and serve food to others.

Many Earthlings work together in __organizations__ called charities. A charity helps people by raising money and giving help to those who need it.

Charities hold events, such as this walk, to raise money and __awareness__.

"Working together is a great way to help others meet their needs."

There are many kinds of charities. Often, a charity helps a certain group or tries to solve a certain problem. Some charities help Earthlings who lost their homes. Others help Earthlings who are sick.

Some charities give Earthlings temporary shelters.

Some charities send doctors, nurses, and medicine to Earthlings in need.

Earthlings who have a lot of money can give large amounts of money to charities. If these Earthlings are also famous, they can get many other Earthlings to pay attention to the charity too.

Charities need to raise money to help others. Some Earthlings donate, or give, money to charities.

DONATE

DIAMOND BALL

cL

clara lionel foundation

E DIAMOND BAL

Rihanna is a famous Earthling who created her own charity. It helps children go to school. It also helps Earthlings recover from natural disasters.

MANY WAYS ★ TO HELP

Donating money is not the only way to help others. Earthlings can give their time too. They can help others solve a problem. They can volunteer to work at a charity.

"Bo. I have an idea that could solve your problem."

"Okay, fine. Will you help me, please?"

Earthlings can also help by donating goods such as food, clothing, and toys. These items can be given to those who need them, or sold to raise money.

"You could donate your extra things to charity. That will help get rid of the mess!"

"That's a good idea."

Earthlings can volunteer to help run charity events. These events can help raise money or send a message. Events can make other Earthlings aware of an issue. There are different kinds of events.

Bake sales

BAKE SALE TODAY!

Talent shows

Charity runs

Working together lets Earthlings run events and help many others. But one Earthling can help others on his or her own too. Small actions can make a big difference.

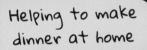

Helping to make dinner at home

Helping a friend learn to read

LET'S GET GIVING!

Helping others makes Earth a better place to live.

"Now I know how Earthlings help each other. But why do they help others?"

"Earthlings like to help each other. Helping others helps everyone meet their needs. It feels really good to help others."

How can you help others and make your <u>community</u> a better place to live? To get started, think about answers to these questions. Write down all of your ideas.

- Who are some people in need in my community?
- Will I give time or money to a charity? Which one?
- How could I send a message about people in need?
- What goods could I donate?

BO AND ZOP HELP EACH OTHER

Bo and Zop learned that all Earthlings need help sometimes. It is important to know that asking for help is okay.

Asking for help is always a good idea!

Bo has learned to ask for help, and Zop feels great because he helped his friend. Bo learned a lot about charities. He even decided to sell some of his old toys and clothes to raise money for charity. Now he needs to decide which one!

GLOSSARY

awareness   Having or showing knowledge about something

basic   Simplest or most important

community   A group of people who live, work, and play in a place

donate   To give something away for a cause, such as charity

Earthlings   Human beings

goods   Things people make

natural disasters   Events in nature that cause damage or harm to humans

organizations   Groups of people with common goals

poverty   Not having enough money to pay for important thing

satellite   A human-made object that circles Earth or another space object

temporary   Not permanent

volunteer   To offer to do something for free

INDEX